Wild Spirit
of the
Living God

Prayer Poems
for the Journey

Russ Parker

What people are saying about...

Thank heavens for Russ Parker, a contemporary voice in the great biblical and spiritual tradition of prayer poets.
Michele Guinness
Writer and Broadcaster, Author of Child of the Covenant

Whatever, and wherever, your journey, these poems will become companions – and some of them, friends.
Rob Parsons
Director of Care for the Family

Those who want to slow down, and speak and listen to God again, will find in these prayer-poems a very helpful resource. Whether our problem is too few or too many words, these heart-felt thoughts of Russ Parker will give us the simplicity and space to encounter the Lord at last in the deep places.
Revd Dr Jeanette Sears
Author of 'Murder with Mr Rochester'

I have been personally blessed, inspired, convicted, challenged and comforted by Russ' exquisitely crafted prayer poems.
Bishop Eric Pike
Author of; 'Who do you say I am?' A personal Response to Jesus' Question.

Russ has a wonderful understanding of the struggles of our rugged humanity, and through these prayers he gives language to some of our deepest heartfelt longings and dreams, drawing us into a closer love for the God who hears every prayer.
Michael Mitton
Author of *Restoring the Woven Cord* and *Seasoned by Seasons*

These poems are dangerous and need to be handled with prayer. Some are sharp as scalpels exposing thoughts and intentions of our hearts to our discomforted gaze. I can give no greater commendation for this book, than to say; " Read it, dwell in it, feed on it, and you will know the treasure of his heart." You could also discover a gateway into the eternal.
Eric Delve
Author of To Boldly Go!

These aren't poems to peruse, but words that will grab your heart and lead you to worship the awe-inducing Father, the risen and life-giving Christ, and the wild and wonderful Spirit. Russ gives us the poetry that will spark our imaginations and fill our hearts with wonder and love. A resource to use individually and with others - I know I'll take it on retreat with me. Don't miss this faith-building gift.
Amy Boucher Pye
Author of Finding Myself in Britain

There is something of the holy fool about Russ Parker: someone who is willing to live on the edge and say things as they are, however raw and uncomfortable that might sound. Indeed, these are some of the most honest prayers that you are likely to come across in the Christian community right now, and I thank God for them, as well as the delightful liturgies at the end.

Ian Stackhouse
Senior Pastor of Millmead Baptist Church, Guildford

Dedication

I dedicate this anthology to my wife Roz who was the very first person I had the courage to read my poems to.   She has always believed in me even when I was in no position to do so myself.

Contents

Foreword by Michele Guinness

The Wild Spirit

Healings on the Journey

Easter Risings

Hunger

Pathways

Rites of Passage

Foreword

We are not as imaginative in prayer as we could be. It often seems, both in my own prayer life, and in the extempore communal prayers of the church, that inspiration gives way to a jumble of rambling phrases. Yet the Scripture writers, from Moses to the Psalmist, the Apostle Paul or the much-loved John, all conversed with the Almighty in some of the most beautiful words and memorable ways available to them. Their prayer poems have stayed with us, fed and sustained us for generations.

So thank heavens for Russ Parker, a contemporary voice in the great biblical and spiritual tradition of prayer poets. Russ is a man for whom prayer matters so much that it must be the very best he has to offer, and that is his poetry, for poetry is the vehicle that best lends itself to expressing the deepest heart cry, the greatest longings, the unfathomable mystery and sudden, overwhelming sense of wonder, grace and glory that fill the human spirit. These poems are fresh and vivid, immediate and alluring.

But be warned, they're not just an easy read.

Russ takes us into the secret place of his own journey with God, and it often feels, as we read them, as if we're treading on holy ground.

Here we will plumb the depths and hit the heights of human experience, and the road from one to the other can be uncomfortable, as the superficial niceness attached to much of the communication that passes for prayer is stripped away and replaced with raw and real emotion.

No one is perhaps better equipped to write in this way than Russ. Both personal experience, and his many years as the Director of the Acorn Christian Healing Foundation, have given him a profound insight into self-doubt and bewilder-ment that afflicts the human spirit. After all, he's a Scouse by background, a child of those swinging sixties in a Merseyside that 89pro-duced a wealth of talented songwriters, dram-atists and poets including Willy Russell and the Beatles. He too has always been a free spirit, unfettered by convention, dissatisfied with the status quo, saddened when human beings are prevented from reaching their God-given poten-tial, all underpinned with a gentle, self-deprec-ating, sense of human. It was in Liverpool he learnt that the dogmas that divide Christians are artificial, that there are lessons to learn from both fiery Protestantism and quiet Cath-olicism, and that the best in both traditions can be invigorating and enriching.
Russ went on to work in a variety of very ordin-ary jobs, made extraordinary by his encounters with people whose lives he touched in his own inimitable way. When his ministry became offi-cial, he never allowed his professionalism or academic prowess to curb his inner freedom or clip the wings of his imagination. He's never less than ruthlessly honest about his own diffi-

cult journey through pain to new joy. Meeting Russ is always a revelation. He never does or says what anyone expects. And he remains one of the best story-tellers I have ever met.

These are the influences that have prepared and polished the gems in this treasure chest. Here are the years of seeking, listening, questioning, doubting, hurting, learning, loving and wondering, of personal soul-searching, and of empathy with the hundreds who have sought his ministry. Here is comfort in pain, encouragement in indecision, support in bewilderment, reassurance in doubt, challenge in self-pity, and a glimpse of the everlasting joy and pace that is there for all the battle weary pilgrims.

Russ stretches our praying beyond where it normally stops. But would the wild, untamed, all-knowing Holy Spirit of God expect anything less than ruthless honesty? He once wrote one of his own inimitable dedications in a book to us, "He is wild, but he won't hurt you." I've never forgotten that phrase. It captures the essence of the Aslan-like God Russ knows, loves and trusts, who takes us by the hand and gently leads us upwards and onwards to some of the scarier, but wonderful places we have never visited before.

There is an almost Celtic flow and rhythm to the prayer poems that make them memorable, so that the more they are read, the more treasure they yield.   Whether they are used publicly or privately, and I will use them for both, they will feed and strengthen us, and make us rethink and revise our own prayer journey.

It takes the creativity of the poet to release our own imagination in prayer. That is Russ's gift to us, for once it happens, we will never be satisfied with anything less.
Michele Guinness
Writer & Broadcaster

Prayers to the Wild Spirit

Wild Spirit, Wild Wind

Lord God of the wild wind of heaven,
Send us your warm wind,
Your fresh wind,
Your mighty wind;
It's what we want for Jesus' sake.
Amen

Vision Prayer

Wild Spirit of the living God
fall afresh on me.
Give me the eye of the eagle
so that I can see what is far off
and pray,
"thy kingdom come nearer,
thy kingdom come more powerfully,
thy kingdom come on earth as it is in
heaven,
thy kingdom come now."
Amen

Restoration

Wild Spirit of the living God
be the calm in my storm,
the light in my dark;
the One who believes in me
even when I don't.

Wild Spirit of the raised up Son,
be the healer of my hurt,
the holder of my hand;
the One who seeks better things for me
even when I can't.

Light the lion's flame of passion in me,
give me the giving heart
of heaven's holy warrior
so that I learn to be still,
to be stopped,
to recover,
to be released,
to be renewed
through Jesus Christ,
the bloodied but victorious lamb.
Amen

Servant Heart

Wild Spirit of the living God,
breathe the breath of heaven's lion
into this timid soul of mine.
Shape me by the touch of the crucified
lamb,
so that I carry the cross
with the dignity of a crown.
Wrap my fears in the faith you have in
me,
and help me to lean into your blowing
winds,
stand in the gaps of your calling,
fall under the weight of grace,
speak to mountains in your name,
go quietly to the secret place of prayer,
give away my gifts that others may grow
and in steps hardly noticed,
be changed forever into your likeness
through Jesus Christ my Lord.
Amen

The Path I Tread

Wild Spirit of the living God,
bless to me the path I tread,
when I should stop
and where I should go;
let your welcome presence
help me to know
the time to be silent,
the time to scream.
Let there be places
where I can doubt and dream.
Let these be moments
when I am shaped as a true child
of the scarred and wounded king.
Amen

Dreamer's Prayer

Wild Spirit of the living God,
Make a dreamer out of me.
Step into my sleep
And call me to new adventures
On the tides of your turning grace.
Let my night times
Be changed and charged
With the dawning day of new insights.
Let my resting in the dark
Lead to dancing in the blazing morning
Of new revelations of the depths
And layers of your care
For the whole of me,
Sleeping and awake.
Let the ending of the day
Lead to glimpses
Of one like the son of man
Whose face is like the shining sun
In all its brilliance.
Amen.

The Rhythm of Renewal

O Holy Spirit of the living God,
In my life
Be wild and free;
Uphold me and upset me,
Strengthen me and weaken me,
Stop me and stir me,
Waken me and rest me,
Teach me and test me,
Make me more like Christ,
Make me fully human,
Whether it be the cross or the crown
May your mercy and your might
Flood me and fill me
So that I long for God all the more.
Amen

I Want to See You

Wild Spirit of my nights and days,
wake me up with your word of life
so that I might see you,
so that I might serve you.

Jesus Christ, bright and morning star
shine on the highways of my heart
so that I might see you
so that I might serve you.

Great God of waiting and wonders
weave your threads of healing in me
so that I might see you,
so that I might serve you,
so that I might celebrate you,
my Lord and my God.
Amen

Growing Up, Going On

Wild Spirit of the living God,
Teach me to go through life
The right way around,
To be so secure in who I am rather
Than in what I do.
Give me moments of cradling quiet
So that I can be restored.
Let me hear your lion's roar
And fill my heart with exaltation.
Be the still small voice for me
So that I come out of shadow
Into your sunshine.
Heal the hurting child in me
So that I can go on growing up
And live in the power of your Kingdom
presence.
Amen

Being There

Wild Spirit of the living God,
Make me cool waters
In someone else's parched land;
A sheltered place for the fallen
A haven for the wounded;
A safe place for the frightened
A highway for the wanderer;
A still place for the fugitive
A home for the weary;
A strong place for the feeble
And a hill for the ones who want to see
further.
Wild Spirit of the living God,
Give me a listening heart instead of an
informed mind
So that I meet someone else's need
Rather than my own,
Through Jesus Christ my Lord,
Amen

Grab me God

Wild Spirit of the living, breathing God
Come and get me,
Come and grab me,
op Come and get a hold of me.
I don't want to manage without you
anymore.
Wild Spirit of the living, breathing God
Do your deep work,
Do your best work
Do what's in your heart to do,
I don't want the thin, unchallenged life
anymore.
Wild Spirit of the living, breathing God
Don't go,
Don't leave,
Don't be the unseen observer, silent
listener.
I don't want to be safe but sorry any-
more.
Wild Spirit of the living, breathing God
Send your Spirit,
Send him more powerfully,
Send him now.
I don't want to be anywhere else any-
more.

When a child dies

Wild Spirit of the living God
I know you can see beyond my pain,
Hold the child I have lost today
She comes with the names
We honour her with;
She carries traces of my father
And is named after the grand old mother
Whom I lost so long ago.

I cannot share or teach this child a thing
But she can get an education with Christ
and angels.

The pain feels more than I can bear,
I'm angry and confused,
Stunned that all the things we had
planned
Now stand meaningless
Like an accusing finger pointing at the
absurdity
Of making plans for another's unborn
life.

Everybody tells me that I will have an-
other,
one day,
I know that they are trying to be kind
But I will not give up my grief so cheaply
Or forget her so easily.

Wild Spirit of the living God
I know you can hear and hold my scream;
It is only my ruptured love which
Looks to the man of sorrows to redeem.

Healings on the Journey

I Turn Home

Leader When I am lost and need to find my way...
All I turn home.
Leader When I am hurt and want to find healing...
All I turn home.
Leader When I am at the cross-roads and don't know which way to turn...
All I turn home.
Leader When something wonderful has happened and I want to tell everyone...
All I turn home.
Leader When confused and want to make the right choice...
All I turn home.
Leader When I've made a mess of things...
All I turn home.
Leader When I need to confess...
All I turn home.
Leader When I need to say sorry...
All I turn home.

Leader When I cannot fix the things that are broken...
All I turn home.
Leader When I am ready to give God my best...
All I turn home.
Leader When I am old and giving up more and more things...
All I turn home.
Leader When I am ready for my heavenly homeland...
All I turn home,
I turn home.
Amen

Healing the Land

Lord come and heal our land,
Let there be light in our darkened, soul-
less cities,
Let there be green in our wasted, indus-
trial sites,
Let there be a letting go of our dirty,
scarred memories,
Let there be gardens in the ghettos of
our church's story,
Let there be a loving for the soil from
which I came,
Let there be a neighbour in me for the
nations of the world.
Lord come and heal our land.
Amen

Giftings for Growth

O Lord God, Father in heaven,
Grant me those gifts which help me
grow:
Your still small voice
Which brings me out of my frightened,
Closed down heart.
Fire of sacred love
Which heals what is mine so I hold
What is yours.
The Listening Christ
Who waits on my road of retreat
Turning me home.
Surprising grace
Helping me dig the precious pearl
From the field of dreams.
Amen

The God who Sees More

Lord God of signs and wonders,
When sin has silenced our song,
Sing about the good you still see
In us.

Great Son, friend of all who stray,
When shame has broken our best,
Create a new and living way
For us.

Wild Spirit winged with healing power,
When lies destroy our standing,
Remind us that you share this road
With us.

Therefore
We'll run,
Stagger,
And bow,
then kneel
In penitence
Because you care,
For us.
Amen

Resurrection Sunrise

When I cannot see the end of things,
When the darkness shines brighter than
the sun,
When the wound will not be healed,
When I can see no answer to my ques-
tions;
When I am afraid of being hurt, again,
Fill me with knowing you are there,
For me.
You are the first to weep over shattered
lives,
The wounded healer who mends broken
hearts,
The first to die and rise,
The holy victim who shouts through the
silence,
"It is finished!"
When I am blinded by the power of
present things,
Fix my eyes on you,
The battered God of the cross,
And break the power of my painful days
With reminders of new and better days
Still to come,
Your resurrection sunrise,
For me.

Remember Me

God of the dark and difficult places,
Remember me.

When forgotten,
When friends are strangely silent,
Remember me.

When foolishly I wallow
In broken dreams,
Remember me.
When I struggle

With the unfairness of things,
Remember me.

When I break and lose my way,
and rage and scream,
Remember me.

With my gifts unrecognized
And my life misunderstood,
Remember me.

Help me to see the friends I do have,
Those who listen,

Those without answers
But who can hear My questions.

Those who can touch
But not possess me,

Those not frightened
By the power of my doubting heart.

So weave the lightness of your love
Into the threads of my darkness
And do this in remembrance of me.
Amen

Healing Places

O God of all my healing times,
When I am rushed and racing through,
Find for me,
A place
where I can be still,
A time
To stay in touch with heaven's will,
A mountain
To climb above the things that bring con-
fusion;
A garden
For dialogue and painful decisions;
A place
Where the hearing of your word brings
visions;
A quiet place,
A screaming place,
A healing place
And a holy place.
Amen

God of the Last Chance

God of the last chance,
The next chance,
The only chance,
All Don't let go of me;
Give me another chance.

Son of the shepherd heart,
The broken heart,
The bursting heart,
All Don't let go of me;
Give me new heart.

Spirit of the eagle-eyed vision,
The heavenly vision,
The nightmare vision,
All   Don't let go of me;
Give me renewed vision,
Through Jesus Christ my Lord.
All Amen

Christ Before Me

Lord Jesus Christ,
Holder of the heavens
Who spoke creation into life;
There was a time when you could not
speak,
You have been down my road before me.
Lord Jesus Christ,
Walker among angels
Who rescued the bruised and the broken;
There was a time when you were car-
ried,
You have been down my road before me.
Lord Jesus Christ,
Robed in glory, crowned,
There was a time when you were hidden,
You have been down my road before me.
When I am speechless, be my living
word,
When I cannot stand, be my strong sup-
port,
When I run and hide, be my one true
friend.
Amen

What God Hears

The prayer of the lonely
Which pierces the clouds,
The cry of dereliction
Which electrifies the crowds;
The song in the shadow
Which holds hope still,
The weeping of the beaten
Who have had their fill;
The anger of the abused
Which is long overdue,
The strangled heart
Of those who can't make do;
The pain of the robbed
Who feel diminished,
The power of the weak
Who feel they are finished;
The silence of the lamb
Who stands condemned,
And the roar of the lion
Whose endless life transcends,
Overcomes and undoes
The twisted darkness of
Our unhealed wounds
So that he can tell us
We are healed and held
And loved to the very end.

Easter Risings

The Executioner's Art

Jesus waits
For the executioner's skill
To be delivered
In the silence of an
Effortless business drill.
The easy calm of the craftsman as he
Carefully caresses the cross,
Checking where the victim's foot will
Rest, and shaves off and planes down
Strips of wood;
With his whetted thumb he runs it along
The beam to make sure It is at its best.

His practised eye gauges the height
Of the man waiting for his finished work
And adjusts the stock to hold his body,
Alive and dead weighted.
He tosses the nails over in his palm,
Measuring their length and picking
The best ones to pin his feet in place.
His patience is an art and none of it is
Lost on the battered carpenter who
Would be the first one to taste his Fin-
ished skill.

The killing calm
Of the soldiers, idling as they do,
Gazing at their prisoner
With a practised dismissal;
Cracking jokes and lying as usual
About the women they've had.
It's their way of dealing with reminders
Of the disfiguring they're about to do
And bend this man out of shape and
stretch him apart so his mother wouldn't
even recognize him;

After all,
They are only going to work.

The tortured calm
Of the relatives
Bunched together like stalks of corn,
Holding on to each other
Out of nameless fears;
Feeling powerless,
Dreaming impossible rescues.
And Jesus the victim,
Is not silenced but still;
He is the only one
Who has come to terms
With the bloody mess
On the side of the hill.

Ending of Days

Therefore, as the times of life go by you,
Deep peace of the ever present King be
yours.

When you remember all those unfinished
things,
Deep surrender to the Easter Christ be
yours.

When good- byes and endings are yours
to say,
Deep words of the Holy Son be yours.

When the moment of letting go is yours
to give,
Deep holding of heaven's shining Lord be
yours.

When there is nothing else to say or to
be done,
Deep speech of the one who says "Come
up here,
and see what must be," be yours.
Amen

Christict on the pavement

You spilled your blood on the pavement
Long before you got to the cross.
You heaved your heart through the sad
streets
Where your mother dizzily stood
And the crowd bayed for your blood.
It seemed only a moment ago
That you were their champion
And they just loved the show.
They hung on your every word's cry,
But now it's you they want hung out
To dry,

But the wounding was in you long before
this,
When you had been rejected by the very
ones you kissed.
When your mother thought you were
mad
And your brothers said you'd been had,
And they left you with your disciples
Who fell like ripe apples

When the gangs ganged up on you.

Judas tortured himself into betraying
 you,
Peter couldn't help himself in denying
 you;
The rest of the men simply vanished
from view.
Yet you are not surprised by our fickle
lives
And the ease with which our deep
devotion
Melts so easily and trickles
away.

Not so you,
You abide,
You remain true,
You do not lose yourself
When the darkness closes in.
Even in the dark
when your public had lost interest
and scrambled for safe cover,
And the band had ceased to play
And the last punter
had trailed home to his bed;

Until only you remain,
Alone, intact, in pain,
Stabbed but generous,
Hanging on in there because
You were there for us.
You held our mess
And in our place
Paid the price for our release.

The View from Here

The view from here is terrific.
There are rank upon ranks of dazzling
Bright angels whose shimmering wings
Catch rainbows as they glide before the
Ancient of days.

Mighty beasts bow to the punctured
Lamb and heaven's holy Warrior strokes
The flanks of a purring Lion.   Wise ones
and golden unicorns Hush heaven's wild
party when they fall Before our shining
Lord and sing his Praises and tell again
the never ending Story.

And I'm rubbing shoulders with Moses
And Mother Teresa, a Welsh bishop
Whose name I can't pronounce and a
School-teacher from Bognor I knew when
I was eight.

You see further than your dreams have
Dared,
God is bigger than you have heard.
You can play leap-frog to your heart's
Content and watch Jesus make straight
Everything that was bent.

The view from here is fantastic.
I've listened to hump-back whales as
They prayed.   I've watched the lame as
They walked around all day,
Laughed when the blind could believe
Their eyes.
This is the place where all unfinished
Stories have better endings:
The never born are named,
The unwanted are celebrated,
The forgotten are remembered,
And the aborted are baptised in crystal
Waves.
Together they sing songs that cheer the
Heart of the wise.

And guess what?
The other moment I bumped into that
Couple from our fish and chip shop,   and
They're still smelling of crispy batter
And hot Pukka pies.

You see further than your dreams have
Dared,
God is bigger than you have heard.
You can play leap-frog to your heart's
Content and watch Jesus make straight
Everything that was bent.

The view from here is out of this world.
When you think of my final battles which
Left you low, well you should see what I
Can do now.

I'm not breathless anymore and I can
Scan a universe in Technicolor;

I've got a radiant shimmer and a see-
Through glow that's to die for.

I swim alongside starfish with names that
You don't know and I cuddle giant Pandas
As we roll over in the snow.

I'm bursting with the pleasure of Heav-
en's high lover whose hold on me Has
stayed my course and called me so Much
higher.

I'm seated in the heavens but I can see
aAl the way home to you,

I'm kneeling with millions around a
Saphired throne and the sigh of our
Prayers is waking up worlds.

So be pleased for me and let me go
And when the angel trumpets your time
To fly, come and find me in the dance of
Darlings waiting in the sky.

You see further than your dreams have
Dared,
God is bigger than you have heard.
You can play leapfrog to your heart's
Content and watch Jesus make straight
Everything that was bent.

The Shapes of the Cross

Scream

What was that I heard you say
As you screamed at the God who you
Thought
Had gone away?
Weren't you
Scarred long before the hill?
Deserted by your Peters
Supported by so few.
What were you thinking
As they bloodied you for more?
Was this worse
Than what you bargained for?
You dug deeper than most
When the beam slumped
Into the hollowed groove
Of the executioner's stump.

Nakedness

You hung naked
As the day you were born
But offered your Paradise home
To a thief bound and staked.
Like the emperor with no clothes
You were paraded with false praise
But I think you prayed for them
Who gambled for your seamless cloak.

Powerlessness

Your enemies waited
Until it was hard to speak
When they poured out taunts
And dared you down from your peak.
Was it a moody silence
You were wearing
Or the steadied gaze
Of someone who knew more than he was
saying?

Darkness

It was in the dark you did your best,
Instead of holding it all against us
You said forgive and
Your father did the rest.

How short sighted
The sight of you makes me,
Where I thought we had you caught
Was where you came to set me free.
When you pierced the air
With your finished shout
I thought it was all over,
But you had only just begun.

Song of Saddleworth Moor

They tell me that your rage has kept you
alive.
Are you sure that you are alive?
Your face is lined with aching loss
And each grieving cut begs the question,
"It's not fair!
Where was God when the children
were bundled into the soft peat
on the grimy rims
of Saddleworth Moor?"

Like a deranged animal
Caught in a trap,
You lash and kick out at everything.
You cannot be comforted
Until you are finally done,
Until you have put it all down
And have told your darling child's story
And you finally know that you have been
heard.
What compelling power and shocking
beauty there is
As you bellow out in your pain and rage,
"Where was man, never mind God,
on Saddleworth Moor?

Stabbed inside your heart
Is the unfinished song
of the never to be teenaged
Lesley Anne whose dreams are long
gone,
Stolen and broken and stuffed into the
sloppy turf
Of Saddleworth Moor.
Someone's got to keep her story alive
But it has come at a high price.
Who will sing the songs of those who
cannot?
Who will hold the remembrance of these
things
When we have long gone?
Who will keep the wonders we hoped for
But did not get?
Who is there to stand upon the earth
And celebrate that we were here?
Who is there who knows where the hid-
den children Sleep In their unmarked
beds
On Saddleworth Moor?

Only Jesus,
Only the shattered son of the crucifix;
Bludgeoned out of shape,
Tortured and ritually disfigured,
Each segment of his abused cycle of dy-
ing
watched over by unfriendly, distant eyes,
until he was silenced into the ground.
Who triumphed over the numbing an-
onymity of death
And delayed his resurrection destiny long
enough
To terrorize and dethrone all the hopes
of hell,
And emerge singing our silenced songs;
Picking us up where we had fallen
So we could join in with the chorus
And finish our songs around a throne of
witnesses
On Saddleworth Moor.

*This poem was inspired by watching a TV dis-
cussion on forgiveness between Gordon Wilson,
whose daughter Marie was killed by an IRA
bomb at Enniskillen, and Ann West whose
daughter, Lesley Ann Downey, was murdered by
Myra Hindley and Ian Brady. Gordon Wilson had
immediately offered forgiveness to his daughter's killers and this triggered the rage in Anne
West.*

Confessing unhealed history

We stood in a circle

Riveted to the hold of history,

Captured by the legacy

Of what we all had done.

And we heard a voice crying through

"I will remember them,

I will heal them too."

And I joined my words of lament

To those who stood with me

And I knew that this was Calvary

Where Jesus cried, "It is done!"

Mary's Song

This Mary has sat here many times quite
still,
Her face fixed, concentrating as the ac-
tion unfolded.   The
seriousness of years etched into her far-
away gaze   As
she cast her mind back through the moments which have sculptured her life.

That Mary has also been on a journey,
From the dizzy rush of angel chorused
motherhood
To the greedy madness of Calvary's
wood.
From cradling her dangled, dead son
with a mother's "why?"
To being closeted in a hushed and
crowded room waiting for the news that
death had finally died.

This Mary could be mistaken for being
sad as she weaves her slender fingers
In a rosary of prayers.
But if we open our eyes a little wider

And look beyond the appearance of
things,
We will see her cut a smile of wonder
As she slowly triumphs over the weight
of years.

That Mary is sitting wrapped up in God
As she hums the list of important songs
Of glories that have come by and gone.
From the silence of her first born
shrouded in darkness,
To the roar of victory piercing worlds
with forgiveness.
From mothering her son from playtime
to manhood,
To the embraced surrender of Golgotha's
brutal wood;
But not before he looked down to see
her there and give her another son who
would care for her.

This Mary is that Mary in all of us.
She sat and waited in an upper crowded
room for the Spirit and the sparks to fly;
We too wait for hope to come and take
the shape of the risen Jesus.

For many years I conducted a weekly Holy Communion service at Whitehill Chase in Hampshire which was the home of the Acorn Christian Healing Foundation. The Mary in this poem came regularly and she battled her way through depression with the help of the deep love she had for Jesus. She inspired me to never give up hoping in God for new and better days.

Give me Jesus

Hunger

O God of everything that really counts,
I give to you my best;
The glossary of achievements which oth-
ers sing out,
The shiniest miracle on which I dine out,
Possessions which I share out,
Blessings which your grace gives out,
My most important assets which I hold
out;
Still give me the Spirit's power to want
you more
So that I count all these as loss,
Only, give me Jesus.

O God of all life's challenges,
When I lose the thing I hoped for,
Break the life I longed for,
Squander the talent I was shaped for,
Forget the dreams I was born for,
Neglect the callings I was saved for,
Drown in failures I didn't bargain for;
Still give me the Spirit's fire to trust you
more
So that I press on,
Only, give me Jesus.

O God of all bright endings,
Whose stunning face we will all get to
see,
And be dazzled by the daring of your
eternity,
Where martyrs stripped of shape and
substance
Are welcomed into their homeland
haven.
Whose tiger-like, Calvary striped roar
Will deaden the assembled might of the
hordes of Hell.
Whose return will clutter the sky
With air-born saints and congregations of
angels
And blasting trumpets crescendoed
With some archangel's immaculate
shout,
And even though I want it all now;
Still give me the Spirit's passion to love
you more
So that I eagerly await your appearing,
Only, give me Jesus.

Prayer for Holy Hunger

O God,
I have tasted your presence
And it has both satisfied me
and made me thirsty for more.
I am conscious of my need for you,
But not conscious enough.
I am ashamed of my lack of desire.
I want to want you more.
I long to be filled with longing for you.
I thirst to be made even more thirsty.
Give me a glimpse of you
So that I will want to gaze for longer.
Show me your glory so that I may know
you,
In your mercy begin a new work of love
in me,
Get me out of my comfortable compla-
cency
And be filled with desire for you,
In Jesus' name,
Amen

I Want!

God,
I don't want to play at being strong,
I want to go weak
I want to belong
I want to go low,
I want to be in the place where you
speak.
I don't want deeply, meaningful absence
I want the irrepressible
I want disturbance
I want to go low,
I want the God of the impossible.
I don't want a tame holiness,
I want the wild Spirit
I want God's restlessness
I want to go low,
I want you to get closer than this.
I want
I want
I want you,
God

Make it Loud

I cried aloud to God,
Not one of your controlled
And measured speeches;
But one of those loud enough
To make people think you're having a
Breakdown,
Or you're somebody who's a problem
And needs to be taken away, quickly and
Quietly.
Don't give me this "I am only a whisper
away"stuff,
I don't want to gingerly spoon out
My heart to you but scream up a tantrum
Of needing you;
I have to get it out and get it out still
More.
Don't mistake this for self-pity,
Self-pity is a form of recreation I am
Hopeless at.
I'm not feeling sorry for myself;
I'm giving myself a hard time so I don't
Settle for less than knowing
The full blown version of you.

First Signs

When what I have will not do,
When invitations to pray feel about as
Appetising as the shipping news.
When I'm tired with the God I think I
Know.
When I can't stand that latest
Everybody's singing it song,
When people go down in the Spirit and I
Go out bored.
When testimonies sound like speeches at
The Oscars;
When worship feels like I'm partnered
With a chorus of overweight dancers.
When I want to punch the next person
Who tries to fix me and sort me out.
When I prefer sermons to conversation,
When I smile too much.
When I prefer to be skeptical about Mir-
acles and buy books written by Mystics
but fall asleep reading the Foreword.
When I can't be surprised anymore.
When I scream, "God, there's got to be
More than this!" When there is no more
Fun in doing this;   Then it's time to get
Desperate for Jesus.

Just for Once

Just for once,
Let's not have that type of revival
Which is more about being in charge
again
Than about being broken open
And poured out in the care of worlds.
Rather, let it be the Spirit of healing say-
ing,
"God is back
Giving the kiss of life
To a world turned pale and dull."

Just for once,
Let's not have that kind of worship
That's more about indulging ourselves
Than chasing after the illusive God
Who jumps on us from his hide and seek
heart
And shows us little things to wonder our
lives
And keep us chasing after him for years.
Just for once,
Let's not have that kind of report on the
world's problems
Which robs me of my passion and re-
duces me to tears

Than the one that tells me how we are
surrounded by
Lonely, angry, out of shape, hurting kids
Still waiting for the mending hands
Of a broken father's heart.

Pathways

Waiting on God

In stillness,
Like the early morning air
Before the birds
Awake to dawning light;
In tempests,
Tossed about with angry moods,
Teach me to listen
And discover your word to meet my
need.
When I'm broken,
When I'm brittle,
When I'm confused,
When I'm cornered,
When I struggle
To find the right path;
Teach me to listen
And find the way forward from my need.
Through our Saviour Jesus Christ,

Amen.

Choose the Road

Lord, bless to me the path I tread,
When I should stop,
Where I should go.
Help me to know
The time to be silent,
The place to scream.
Teach me to dream
So that I can sing,
As a child
Of the wounded king.
Amen

Invocation

Catch me God, in your generous grace,
Slow me down to your walking pace.
So that I might see you
Walking on my low roads,
Standing at my cross-roads.

Call me God, with your surprising hope,
Make my ordinary way a window for
wonder.
So that I hear you say
"I'm here to restore you
I honour and esteem you."

Keep me God, despite my deep doubt-
ing,
Widen my horizon with new possibilities.
So that I know you
Shining through the everyday
Dazzling me with eternity.

Catch me, O God,
Call me, O God,
Keep me, O God,
Through Jesus Christ my Lord,
Amen.

And God is Greater than this...

I struggle with knowing that God loves me and it gets me down.
All And God is greater than this
I have a huge temper and I wish I did not give in to it so much.
All And God is greater than this
I battle with OCD and want to be a better mum.
All And God is greater than this
I am a bad witness to the Jesus I long to serve well.
All And God is greater than this
I am confused about what my role in the church is.
All And God is greater than this
I am so easily put down and sink into my depression.
All And God is greater than this

Invite more confessions...

Conclusion
O God, you are so immense and we so limited,
We can see only so far and you blink in visions;

74

Therefore we ask that when we stumble and fall
That you remind us that your love is so much greater than our capacity to fail,
And call us out of our dark shadowlands
Into the walk of your hoping light.

Amen

Prayer for Honouring Leaders

We lay hands on you today
Because we want to honour you
And say thank you for the gift
You are to us.
We recognise that it has not always
Been easy for you,
But we want to thank you for staying
With us and helping us to get closer to
God.

We lay hands on you today
Because we want to say sorry
For not appreciating you enough
And failing to realise your worth.
Please forgive us for not supporting you
properly
Or recognising those times when you
needed care;
For so easily listening to your critics
When we should have celebrated you
more.

We lay hands on you today
Because we want to tell you that we are
for you;
That we want to go forward beside you

And serve our great king together.
We realise that you too have your
dreams of where
You want God to take us;
Some have been broken but some have
stayed alive.
And so we lay hands on you now to say,
"let the dreams of God come true for all
of us."

We lay hands on you today
Because we want your heart to be renewed
And your home to be refreshed by the
presence
Of the high King whom you serve.
We honour you as the one whom God has
definitely
Called to be our leader and cure of our
souls,
We recognise that without you being
here
We are not going to be truly whole.
So may the Lord of the church
strengthen our partnership
and take us all to the next level
of seeing his kingdom come through us,
his broken and blessed people.
Amen

Seldom do our church leaders have an opportunity to be prayed for meaningfully by their own congregations.
This prayer is one in which our leaders, clerical and lay, along with their spouses, are invited to stand and come forward for prayer with the laying on of hands.
Therefore the facilitator for this prayer would need to encourage as many of the congregation that wish to, to gather around and share in the laying on of hands.

Faithful One

Leader: You are the faithful one,
All: When we are faithless;

Leader: You are the glorious one
All: When we wallow in shame;

Leader: You are the forgiving one
All: When we have messed up;

Leader: You are the constant one
All: While we are so feeble;

Leader: You are the rock
All: While we drift around;

Leader: You are all in all to us,
You are our solid ground,
You are our heaven and earth,
The King of Kings;
You are the reigning Christ,
The returning Lord,
You are the healing and delivering Sa-
viour
Who gathers all our confessions
and gives them a home.
You are the faithful one

Who turns our world around;

All: The Holy One who helps us dream
again.
O most faithful God,
Thank you for believing in us
And for being there because
Without you we drift and fade
And lose the life for which we were
made.
Amen

Rites of Passage

Litany of Invitation to Holy Communion

Leader: Come to this place, not
because you love God enough,

All: **But because we want to love
Him more.**

Leader: Recognise that you are
welcome, not because you have
earned it,

All: **But because our risen Lord
wills it and wants it.**

Leader; Come lowly into His presence,
Not because God wants to put
you down,

All: **But because in due time Jesus
will raise us up.**

Leader: Receive the healing touch of
Jesus, not because you are not
well,

All: But because we want to live better lives than we do and learn to give our gifts away so that others may grow.

All: Amen

Prayer of Anointing

I anoint you in the name
Of the Father, the Son and
The Holy Spirit.
Send down your Holy Spirit on (name)
And renew his/her life in the service
Of Christ the healer.
Restore them in your love,
Encourage them with your power
And renew them in the Father's image
Through Jesus Christ our Lord.

Amen

Confession for the Healing of Family Stories

Almighty and everlasting God,
Whose will it is to restore all things
In your well-beloved Son,
The king of kings and the Lord of Lords;
Mercifully grant that the family stories
We bring now before you
May receive freedom and healing
Through your most gracious rule.

Where there have been divisions,
Let there be restoration;
Where there are forgotten children,
Let them come home
And find more love in the
Father heart of God;
Where there has been evil,
Break the powers of darkness
And subject them to your righteous rule.
Let the power of your deliverance and
forgiveness
Bring freedom to the guilty and
Renewal of life to us,
Through Jesus Christ, the first-born from
the dead.
Amen

Trinitarian Credal Prayer for Generational Healing

We believe in God above us,
Maker and sustainer of all life.

We believe in God beside us,
Jesus Christ, the Word made flesh.
Born of a woman, a servant of all
Who was nailed to the cross and died
For the forgiveness of everybody's sins,
Both the living and the departed,
Who ascended into heaven
And is alive for evermore.

We believe in God within us,
The holy Spirit of Pentecostal fire
Who is the life-giving breath
Of the church.

This one, triune God, brings healing
And forgiveness to all and His power
Is over the living and the dead.
He will come again in glory
And so we will all forever be together,
United with our triumphant Lord!

Amen

Creed for the One People

All
We believe in one, holy, catholic and
Apostolic people.
We believe in making everyone safe
And sound.

Leader
You love the differences in us,
You inhabit the edges of our ways and
Tears,
Our sharp and sensitive don't go there or
I'll bust your face fears;
You tease out the surprise we can be,
You celebrate each human endeavour
And act of kindness because that is when
You see yourself in us.
You invoke all our diminished hopes
And bring them to full measure again.
You don't stop or give up on us until
We all come home together before the
Maker's throne,
To be cheered and welcomed as the Re-
turning children
Of the once lost family of each other.

All
We believe in making sure we stand on
the same, solid ground.

Leader
You swim in the unchartered waters of
Our hidden stories,
Live in our divided heartlands,
Heal the breakdowns in our border Re-
gion lives.

All
We believe in not rocking the boat.

Leader
You're in the habit of shaking the Found-
ations of the world,
Turning over the tables of our well Dis-
ordered priorities.
You say radical wonders that will be used
Against you,
You are often seen in questionable Com-
pany that puts you in the gossip Columns
of all our dirty minds.

All
We believe in singing from the same
Hymn sheet, making sure we are
Speaking from the same page.

Leader
You read books not yet on our shelves,
Sing songs that find their way into our
Dark and wounded selves,
Woo us with holy whispers to dig us out
Of our dug in hates,
Send text messages to guide us back to
Your homeland heart.
When are we going to believe the same
Way as you?

All
When we breathe the breath of Heav-
en's lion,
When we heal the wounded child in all
Of us,
When we rediscover our capacity to be
Surprised,
When we miss wonder and the Ordin-
ary,
When we stop playing safe,
When we are prepared to be broken
Open,
When we won't settle for less than the
Full blown version
Of you.

We believe...We believe.

Creed for a Holy People

All
We believe in one, holy, catholic and
Apostolic people

Leader
We believe in being better than we are
And reaching out for the star
Of burning brightness
That leads us to the place of burning
Bushes.

All
We believe in being stopped in our
Tracks
And turned aside by God's sneaky Dis-
tractions,

Leader
Only to find ourselves on holy slip roads
Which bring us to our undoing at God's
Thin places.

All
We believe in taking off our shoes on
Holy ground

Leader
Providing that our feet do not smell;

All
We believe in fires that warm us well,

Leader
Providing they don't come with an
Archangel's command.

All
We believe in mountain top Transfigur-
ing,
Where the fire of heaven falls for our
Transforming;

Leader
It's stretching it a bit though to confront
Us with the living dead and ask us to
Listen to what they have said.

All
We believe in Calvary mounts and Hill-
side revelations,
And clues to the power of Christ's Resurrection,

Leader
Providing we can stay awake long enough
And don't build our God-proof shelters
Too tough.

All
We believe that we cannot contain this
Too hot to handle God,
Who wakes us up to see that death has
Been robbed and gives us glimpses of
His glory so we can make new the old,
old story.

Leader
O most holy and overwhelming God,
Give us the desperate desire to be more
Like you.

All
You are the transfigured Lord.
Make us the transformed
Sons of Adam and daughters of Eve.

Leader
By visions of the tender, stroking lion
And the roaring, conquering lamb;
By watching the flight of burning ones
And kneeling at the sound of God weep-
ing;

All
By knowing that when we are between
A rock and a hard place,
Or are in over our heads,
That you paid a huge price for us
That you would sell off the world to get
us back,
Every last one of us,
That you would trade your creation
To bring us all home to your heartland
Heaven.

We believe...We believe.

Creed for a Catholic People

All
We believe in one, holy, catholic and
Apostolic people.

Leader
We believe in being the best dreamers in
Town,
We dream of a world where the broken
And the busted get to reign;
Where we listen to the sermons of the
Numb and the altar calls of endangered
species.

All
We believe in outrageous notions;
That all we do sings of God's breathing,
That God is so for the human race
That he puts up with our chosen,
Self destructive sinning
In order to give us all the chances
We need to change direction
And find our way back to becoming
Truly human.

Leader
We believe in a God who steps into our
dreams and calls us to strange meetings
with other tribes,
Who troubles us enough with his love
that we take risks and live beyond our
comfort zones,
Who calls the church to get off its assets
And find its true heart and then give it
away so others may grow.

All
We don't believe in God possessing us,
His father heart is big enough
To give us room to fight him off,
To tell him to stay out of our sleep
And say no to his mad grace.

Leader
We believe in the Great Son, Jesus,
The butchered blessed redeemer
Whose good news heart saves
All the desperate souls here;
The walking wounded,
The screaming and the silent,
The unwanted and unappreciated,
Victims and their perpetrators,
The wanderers and the waylaid,
The voyagers and the stay at home,

The dreamers and the dammed,
And those who feel they have left no
mark to say that they were here.

All
We believe in the wild, Spirit of God,
Who weaves the wind of God's new
timings into the broken hopes of all our
dreamings.

Leader
We believe in a God who patiently
wrestles with our temptations to settle
for less;
Who won't let us wallow in self-pity but
tells us "You are worth much more than
this!"   He only calls the broken to turn
the world upside down
And insists that only fools need apply.

All
We believe...We believe.

Creed for an Apostolic People

All
We believe in one, holy, catholic and
Apostolic people.

Leader
We believe in always being around as
Well as on the move,
We believe in being absolutely still
And going for it when we can.

We believe in making our presence here
As common as dust,
As ever present as the air we breathe,
As committed as gravity,
As constant as News 24.

All
Then the world might know
We are here,
We're among them,
Mixed up with them,
Settled, camped and remaining here.
Unpacked and looking for room to live
Here;
Mulched in, dug over and manured in
Here.

Leader
The sent out are we,
Wombling is our pedigree,
Underground, over ground, wandering
Free.
We are the people of limited talent,
Broken, busted and bent;
Wondered by the king of dreamers
Emmanuel's peculiar race,
Ordinary people shocked through with
Grace.
Not spiritual tourists on vacation caring
Visiting the reservations of lost souls,
But pilgrims of the long haul God;
Not the passing through people
But the rooted and grounded in the soil
tribe; the ones who are here to stay.

All
This is our high calling
And if we live up to it at all
It is for the love of God,
For the honour of serving;
Because it must be this way,
For this way went our Lord
Of bloodied and bowed glory,
And because there is no other way on
Offer.

No new, big deal because this is the only deal.

We believe...We believe.

About Russ Parker...

Russ is the Founder and Director of 2restore which is a resource for the healing of church wounds and their legacies. Prior to this he was the Director of the Acorn Christian Healing Foundation for 19 years.

He is a co-founder of the Community of Aidan and Hilda whose mother house is situated on the island of Lindisfarne. He is a founder member of the Fellowship of Christ the Healer (USA) and Christian Healing UK which exist to resource leaders of residential healing and healthcare initiatives. He is a co-founder of Wholecare, an initiative to support and resource Christian Healthcare professionals within the National Health Service.

Russ is the author of a number of books including Healing Dreams, Requiem Healing, Free to Fail, Forgiveness is Healing, The Wild Spirit, Visions in the Night, Healing Wounded History and Rediscovering the Ministry of Blessing.

Russ travels extensively around the UK and abroad, lecturing and teaching on issues connected with Christian Healing and Healthcare, Reconciliation and Church Transformation.

He has a post graduate degree in Phenomenology and Theology from Nottingham University in which his thesis was entitled Dreams as a Religious Phenomenon.

Russ was awarded a Doctor of Divinity from Columbia Evangelical Seminary in the United States in recognition of his outstanding contribution to Christian ministry and for his many writings and his teaching abilities. In particular it was given for the standard of scholarship in his book "Healing Wounded History" which is about reconciling peoples and healing places.

He is married to Roz and lives in Farnham, Surrey, England.

47597391R00061

Printed in Poland
by Amazon Fulfillment
Poland Sp. z o.o., Wrocław